Photographing the nude

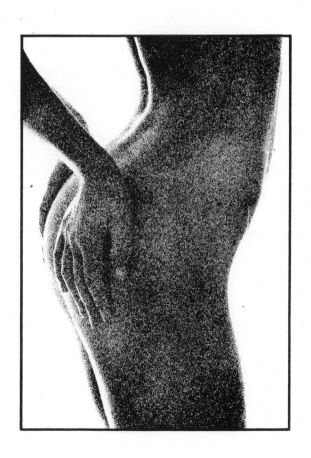

1977 A HARBOR HOUSE BOOK
DISTRIBUTED BY LOUIS J. MARTIN & ASSOCIATES, INC.
95 MADISON AVENUE, NEW YORK, NY, 10016

Editor Jeanne Sullivan
Designed by Janet Sayer
Technical text by Robert Hamilton
History of photography and
interviews by Russell Miller
Illustrations by Keith Palmar

FIRST PUBLISHED IN THE UNITED STATES 1977
by LOUIS J. MARTIN & ASSOCIATES
95 Madison Avenue, New York, NY 10016

Reprinted 1978

ISBN—0-916800-11-3
Library of Congress Card Catalog Number—77-75

Printed in Great Britain

Introduction

The human body, with its infinite variety and flexibility of movement, is a form that has fascinated artists throughout history. In its natural and unclothed state the female body prompted Botticelli to paint his Venus and Picasso to create the *Demoiselles d'Avignon*.

Ever since the craft of photography was introduced a century ago, its practitioners have also been fascinated by the nude form. The challenge still attracts the photographer today, but the techniques the modern photographer uses in nude photography are different from those employed in other areas. *Photographing the Nude* introduces the necessary skills so that anyone who owns a camera can understand them. Whether you want to do natural figure studies, pin-ups or subtle mood shots, this book offers helpful guidance and information. The instructive technical text helps you choose the right camera, film and lenses and there are suggestions for choosing and directing models, for working in natural settings or in a studio, for composing your pictures and for experimenting with a whole range of body shapes.

There are more than 70 photographs in color and black and white to illustrate the text and demonstrate visually how each technique can be used and adapted to a variety of surroundings. In addition, there are interviews with four professional photographers who specialize in nude photography, and their frank discussion and helpful hints are both informative and stimulating.

Contents

Steve Bicknell

A Brief History

From the moment photography was invented, it was inevitable that the female nude would be a subject for the camera. Since the beginning of civilization, artists have found the nude form a subject of endless fascination and challenge; there was no reason to suspect that the early pioneers of photography would think any differently.

The first nude photographs

In 1840, only one year after Daguerre perfected his historic process (commonly known as the daguerreotype) an enterprising Frenchman by the name of Lerebours began taking the first photographs of nudes. His models were professional in every sense of the word—they had to stand still for up to ten minutes while the film was being exposed.

Technical development apart, it is interesting that the creative problems faced by Lerebours are essentially the same as those that have faced every photographer who has ever pointed his camera at a nude. They are enduring problems — how to convey atmosphere, truth and beauty of form with originality.

Aesthetic considerations

Sir Kenneth Clark, the art historian, says that eroticism is always present in the nude. Not so. A number of the best photographers in the world, in their search for individuality, have drawn their inspiration from line and design, from light and shade, not of the entire body but a small part of it. They have seen beauty, and captured it, in the graphics of a single crease in the flesh or the endless permutations of limbs and torso. Eroticism has nothing to do with these pictures, although it exists,

of course, in conventional photographs of the female nude. It becomes art when it is combined with emotion, when the aesthetic qualities of the picture stir the imagination. Sadly, the camera has played an important role in the growth of pornography and so the nude as a legitimate and serious subject of photography is still widely regarded with suspicion. Despite this shadow, few photographers have ever been able to resist, at some time or another, facing up to the formidable problems of photographing the female nude.

Opposite page: Right, an early nude study by Watson, 1856. As with most of the very early photographs of the female nude, the model is shown in a simple, modest pose. Left, this photograph, probably French, 1880, again shows concern for the model's modesty and attempts to copy a classical style pose. This page: Above, many early photographers attempted to emulate paintings. They often built elaborate sets and posed models very deliberately in an effort to make a 'living' copy of an existing painting. This photograph was taken by Richard Polak, about 1914.

Probably the most familiar type of
nude photograph is the pin-up,
several examples of which are shown
on these pages. Throughout the
twentieth century such photographs
have proven to be a popular source
of visual entertainment. Sometimes
provocative, sometimes merely
humorous, they demonstate a wide
variety of photographic styles and
social attitudes.

Early history

In the early beginnings of photography
America, France and Britain were the
first countries to consider nude
photography as just about acceptable,
and then only in certain circles.
Nineteenth-century painters in
France were quick to realize the
value of nude photographs: the
camera was able to capture poses
that no models could hold for long.
Victorian prudery made life more
difficult for photographers in
Britain. Although in society it
was fashionable for women to compile
an album of nude studies of their
female friends (taken by a lady
photographer, of course) most
people were convinced that no decent
woman would take off her clothes
in front of a camera. Those that
did were usually considered to be
prostitutes or pathetic wretches
forced against their will to pose
for their husbands or boy friends.
Most early photographers made the
understandable mistake of trying
to emulate painting. In makeshift
studios they built elaborate
allegorical sets and posed their
models as mythological characters,
often in an attempt to make a
'living' copy of an existing
painting. The results usually only
succeeded in emphasizing the worst
aspects of both painting and
photography.
It was not long, however, before
the realization dawned that
photography could be an art form
in its own right. As soon as this
happened, the days of photographers
simply taking nude pictures of poses
ordered or directed by painters were
over. The photographers found they
had something to say on their own
and a burning desire to say it.
For a time, public morality still
demanded that models in nude
photographs be draped with
strategically placed materials, or
pose lifelessly like the pseudo-
classical statues that were fashionable
at the time: as long as the picture
did not look too much like a real

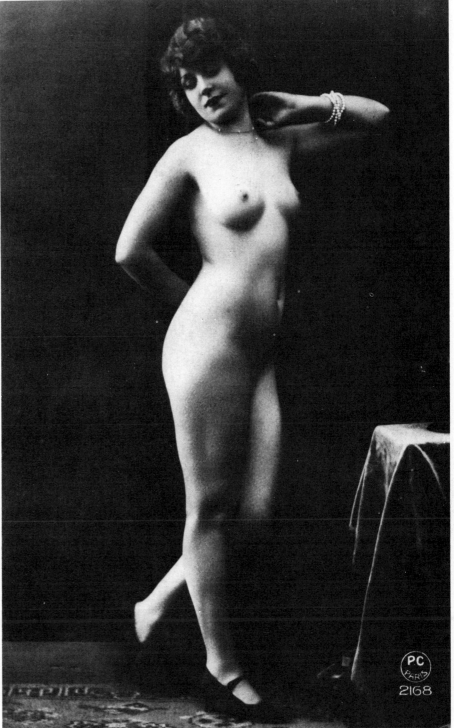

girl with no clothes on, it was all
right. But in 1902 a group of
photographers got together, called
themselves the 'Photo Secessionists',
and dedicated themselves to the task
of getting photography generally
accepted as an art.
The nude photographs they produced
and published in their own magazine
became prototypes for a generation
of photographers. Moody and
romantic, yet balanced by a strong
appreciation of form and design,
they began to show for the first
time some of the vast, unrealized
potential of the camera.

*In the early 1900's pin-up style
photographs became more prevalent.
These two examples, left and right,
are typical of the period.
Models who posed for such pictures were
considered by society to be prostitutes
or women forced into such activities
by their husbands.*

Twentieth-century examples

Following the 'Photo-Secessionists'
came a new wave of photographers
who were to see and picture the nude
in ways never before conceived.
They set out to explore the limits
of the camera and to create pictures

born out of the technique of photography for its own sake. The best known of this new wave was undoubtedly the American, Edward Weston. Using the simplest of equipment — a large view camera, tripod and exposure meter — and natural sunlight, he played a significant part in bringing about today's widespread acceptance of nude photography as a respectable art form.

After Weston, most serious photographers of the nude continued the search for freedom of expression. Bill Brandt, said to be the best British photographer of this century,

even went to the extent of using an old Kodak pinhole camera for nude photography. He felt techniques had progressed so fast that no one had sufficiently explored the possibilities of earlier developments. The sculptural, surrealistic pictures that he did in the 1950's are still regarded as a landmark in the history of nude photography. Perhaps the man most recently responsible for popularizing the nude in photography is Sam Haskins. 'Cowboy Kate', his first brilliant book of evocative, whimsical nude studies, became a best-seller all over the world and inspired the work

of thousands of other photographers. It is the very range of visual possibilities that seem to make the female nude such an attractive subject for photography. This, and the fact that there is still much to be explored within that range.

During the 1950's and 1960's photographs of the female nude formed the basis for many popular mass-media publications. Left and right, the style then tended to be posed and stereotyped, but gradually a wider variety of interpretations became acceptable.

11

Basic Equipment and Film

Choosing the right camera

The choice of a camera is a very personal one, and will depend upon individual needs and the conditions under which the equipment will be used. There is no such thing as the 'best' camera; indeed, there are numberless possible variations in the design of a camera. Before making your choice, you must consider whether you want to use the camera in your hand or on a stand of some sort. Whether you want special focusing and view-finding accessories? Whether you want a built-in light meter? And any other such questions that relate to your needs and circumstances.

Remember, the camera you choose will most likely represent some kind of compromise between economy, flexibility, and quality. No single camera will do every type of job perfectly. Decide first what design will be most useful to you and then what design you are most comfortable working with. It sometimes happens that if you work well with a particular camera, small, technical difficulties can be adjusted and fine pictures can still be taken.

Below, four basic and widely used types of cameras are discussed in more detail.

The single lens reflex camera

Undoubtedly this is the most popular type of camera used today, due to its accuracy in viewing and focusing through the same lens which takes the picture. Exact control over 'parallax' is thus obtained — an important feature in photography of the nude. You will want to know, for example, exactly how the subject's arm follows the line of the body. The single lens will show this *exactly*, while a coupled range-finder type of camera will only show in the view-finder an *approximation* of what is on the negative, however accurate this may be. Other advantages of the single lens reflex (especially on small format models) are the ease of focusing, particularly on moving subjects, and the wide range of interchangeable lenses.

Some single range reflex cameras also have built-in light meters which you can read directly through the lens, enabling one to continually monitor the exposure right up to the moment of pressing the shutter release.

This type of light metering has one important advantage for nude photography. It means that you will not need to break your concentration on the composition of the picture by moving forward to take a light meter reading — you simply do it through the viewfinder. Such a feature must improve the continuity between seeing and photographing. Light metering through the lens should be of the centre-weighted type, as this precludes false readings, from the sky for example.

The single lens reflex also has certain creative advantages. For example, with through-the-lens viewing, should you decide to use a diffuse out of focus foreground you can compose the picture exactly as you want it and select precisely how much of the frame the diffuse area will take up. Remember, too, that with a modern single lens reflex, you view a picture at full aperture, but may, in fact, expose the picture at a smaller lens opening. This can significantly change the shape of an out-of-focus foreground. Make sure in composing the picture, that you view the image at the correct aperture, either with a special 'preview' facility, or with the manual aperture setting. Among the different models of single lens reflex cameras, there is little choice in terms of varying lens and mechanical qualities, but there is considerable choice in terms of general design. If you have large hands for example, you may not find some of the more recently introduced compact models to your liking. On the other hand, these designs normally suit a woman's smaller hands perfectly. Controls should fall naturally beneath the fingers and if you wear glasses, you should still be able to view the full picture area without difficulty. A wide range of interchangeable lenses are available.

The coupled rangefinder camera

The coupled rangefinder camera is generally much quieter than the single lens reflex and also permits very accurate, quick focusing — ideal for working in difficult available light. The only interchangeable lens camera of this type still made in 35mm and using a wide range of lenses is the Leica, and it is considerably lighter and quieter than the single lens reflex.

Another great advantage these discreet cameras have over the single lens reflex is the ability to view the subject continuously and thus see the exact moment at which the shutter release is pressed. For some people this more than compensates for the lack of a built-in device which will correct parallax. In fairness one must add that Leicas do have a very accurate bright line frame in the viewfinder which includes the picture area taken and adjusts for close focusing. The latest Leica M5 also features through the lens light metering, the only coupled rangefinder camera to include this feature. Non-interchangeable 35mm lenses for coupled rangefinder cameras are available in a near infinite number of variations, some featuring fast, semi-wide-angle lenses as standard equipment.

The twin lens reflex camera

This is a versatile camera useful for all kinds of photography. It combines continous reflex viewing, even during the moment of exposure (a separate viewing lens being mounted over the taking lens) and the large 6cm x 6cm (2¼ inch square) negative size.

Twin lens reflex cameras are quiet, capable of fine quality photographs as a result of their larger picture size, and with the introduction of 220 size film are no longer limited to 12 pictures per film. Their disadvantages are their rather bulky size, non-interchangeable lenses in the cheaper models, and waist-level viewfinding. (Eye-level viewfinders are available for some types but these increase the camera's size even more.) As well as having a waist-level viewfinder, the photographer is also viewing the subject the wrong way around and this is another factor to accommodate. Also, on most models, parallax error must always be allowed for. But whatever the limitations of the twin lens reflex it did not stop the French photographer Lucien Clergue from making some of the finest pictorial explorations of the female form! Twin lens reflex cameras, such as the Mamiyaflex, have now pioneered interchangeable lenses, and these are reliable cameras with fine ranges of lenses. They also focus extremely closely and have provisions for parallax correction.

The large format view camera

If your approach is meticulous and studied and you are interested in the fineness of detail offered by a large format (5 inches x 4 inches to 8 inches x 10 inches) this is the type of camera for you. They are expensive, although often reasonably priced secondhand view (also known as 'field') cameras can be found in photo stores. Bill Brandt, one photographer to make a great impact on nude photography in the late 1950's, discovered an old view camera with a very wide angle lens in a secondhand store which had been used by the police to show the whole of a room they were working in. The pictures of nudes he took with this camera are now classics.

The large format view camera is particularly useful for learning fundamental photographic techniques. A wide range of interchangeable lenses are available and film is kept on separate plates rather than in rolls. But it must be mounted on a stand, so it is cumbersome and unsuitable for work with moving objects.

Interchangeable lenses

Working in 35mm, a combination of the 28mm wide angle and the 135mm telephoto, together with the 50-58mm standard lens, will cover almost every effect you will want to achieve in nude photography. Due to its great depth of field, the wide angle is a lens used essentially to see subject and setting with equal clarity. It is

The 28mm (f3.5) wide-angle lens. Manufacturers often recommend it for artistic photography.

The 50mm (f1.4) standard lens. The lens to use for all-round colour or black and white photography.

The 135mm (f3.5) telephoto lens. A must for hand-held photography of distant subject matter or portraits.

COURTESY OF ASAHI PENTAX/RANK PHOTOGRAPHIC

KIM SAYER

useful for photographing the nude, either indoors or out.

The standard lens is most underrated; it is more selective than the wide-angle, and with its high speed and lack of distortion can be a useful tool. A high speed lens means that one can open the aperture all the way up to f 1.4 and hence use the lens in low light situations. With a lens such as the 135mm telephoto, this is not possible, as the aperture can

only be opened to f 2.8 or f 3.5. This medium telephoto 135mm lens is useful for taking close-up pictures of the subject, where you do not want to distort facial features. It is also useful in outdoor work where its slight flattening effect can help you to place a figure within a landscape. The extremely shallow depth of field can also be used to isolate the figure or bits of the figure from the landscape.

Light meters

If the camera you have chosen does not have a built-in light meter, you will need a good one. There are two standard types, each based on a particular kind of light-sensitive cell. One uses selenium, an element which generates a tiny electric current which varies in strength according to the brightness of the light falling on it. The Weston is a particularly good example of this type of meter. It is generally very accurate and sensitive enough for normal situations. The Weston is also capable of taking both reflected and incident light meter readings. This simply means that in normal use the reflected light is measured from the subject at which the meter is pointed. By placing a translucent diffuser over the selenium cell and pointing the instrument at the lens of the camera, you can measure the light which falls — or is 'incident' — upon the subject.

The second kind of meter is the cadmium sulphide meter which uses cadmium sulphide, a 'semi-conductor', as a light sensitive material. This means that if light is shone into the cell as an electric current is passing through it, the resistance — and hence the current — in the cell will vary according to the brightness of the light. These meters are much more sensitive than the selenium type, and the best of them are considerably more expensive than the Weston. Two which can be highly recommended are the Lunasix 3 and the Metrastar. There are a great many others also on the international market, less expensive than these two and just as capable of fine performance.

Basic additional equipment

A good **tripod** will be an essential piece of equipment whenever long exposures are required. Points to look for are: rigidity when the tripod is erect; a ball and socket head which will rotate freely and lock instantly and positively in any desired position; the flexibility to adapt to difficult positions, e.g. very low angles; and a quick release head for removal of the camera. Whenever you want to travel light, a small **clampod** which can be easily carried anywhere is most useful. Work with any type of tripod will also require a fairly long **cable release.**

A small **portable electronic flash,** suitable for use in the studio, is another addition for your camera bag. Features to look for are: sufficient power for your needs (check the guide numbers to determine this); rapid recycling time after each flash; some provision for both battery and mains operation; a wide angle light diffuser at least large enough to cover the field of view of a wide angle lens; and in the case of some of the latest models, computerization. This last is a built-in cadmium sulphide light sensor which in a split second, adjusts the amount of light given off by the flash, according to the distance of the subject from the camera.

Finally, a complete selection of **gelatin filters** will be useful to cover most lighting conditions you may meet. A specific list can be found in the section on filters.

Black and white film

Speed is the first factor to consider when choosing a film. Films which produce photographs with the highest definition and a complete range of grey tones require a considerable amount of light falling on them. For this reason they are called 'slow' films; they have a low rating. 'Fast' films (with a high rating) need less light to produce an image on the film emulsion, but the basic chemistry of these emulsions leads to coarser definition and a narrower tonal range.

In photography of the nude, the emphasis will be on the quality of definition and the resolution of fine textures. Choice of film, then, will be related to the quality of definition required for the size of print you require.

High speed and medium speed film

With the increased emphasis on the use of available light for shooting, many photographers frequently use high speed films, such as Kodak Tri-X or Ilford HP4, as they are suitable for almost any situation. With accurate exposure and good processing, they will also produce fine quality pictures. Good enlargements can be made up to 12 inches x 15 inches from 35mm negatives of high speed films.

However, despite their adaptablilty they are not the right type of film to use for all picture-taking situations. For instance, in a 10 inch x 12 inch enlargement of a high speed film, the grain will be very evident. If you do not want such a grainy effect, it is preferable to use a good quality, medium speed film, such as Kodak Plus X or Ilford FP4. With these films you can sacrifice a single stop of light (by exposing the film at f 2 instead of f 2.8) and make enlargements of significantly finer quality.

Using a medium speed film in the same lighting situations as you would use for a high speed film will need a bit more care. The need for a slightly wider aperture will require more careful focusing to accommodate the narrower depth of field, and the slower shutter speed will mean that you must have a steadier hand. The results, however, will be that much finer (less grainy) than one could achieve with a fast speed film. Sometimes, of course, you will want to have a grainy image, especially if you are trying to create a moody, misty picture. Be sure to decide on the effect wanted before you make your choice.

Slow speed film

Truly remarkable results, particularly from miniature negatives, can be obtained from very slow, fine grain films, such as Kodak Panatomic-X or Ilford Pan F. The slowness of these films means, however, that there is more margin for error in your picture taking. If you are not particularly experienced, you will probably get the best results using them outdoors or by using a tripod under artificial light conditions. These fine grain films are usually in the 50-64 ASA speed rating and should be exposed and processed with great care to obtain the best results. Certain developers will effectively give a higher ASA rating to work with, but to obtain the ideal combination of ultra fine grain and long tonal scale, these films are best developed at the rating intended by the manufacturer. The reason for this is that the films have an inherently high contrast, which is exaggerated by exposing and processing them as if they were higher speed films; for the grainy result which this produces one might just as well use a faster film. It is possible to produce high quality prints — indistinguishable from larger film formats — by processing slow, fine grain film in a D76-type developer, diluted with equal parts water, or in one of the new high 'acutance', or high definition, developers such as Acutol.

Super high speed film

For pictures with lots of action, you may want to try using one of the super high speed films, such as Kodak 2475 or Agfa Isopan Record. These are rated by their respective manufacturers at ASA 1250 and ASA 1000. On their instructions for the film, Kodak say that it is ideal to use for law enforcement photography, which will give some idea of the limits to which the film can be pushed. With this type of film it is important to take careful note of the developer combinations recommended by the manufacturer, as its extreme speed may sometimes make it unsuitable for processing in conventional developers. For most situations that you will want to photograph, it would be preferable to use a film such Tri-X or HP4 (see above) and to process it with a developer such as Acuspeed. This method will have the effect of safely trebling the normal speed of the film, with minimal loss of tone and sharpness. For speeds beyond this limit, use a super high speed film.

Colour

The first essential in selecting a colour stock is to choose a film type to suit the lighting conditions you will be working with. Colour emulsions are designed to be used with lighting of specific 'colour temperatures'. This is a complex concept based on the colour of light radiated by a theoretical, perfect light-source. Practically, all this means is the higher the colour temperature, the bluer the light; the lower the colour temperature, the redder the light.
Colour temperature is measured in units called degrees Kelvin (°K). Daylight is about 6,000°K, and tungsten light, conventionally, is 3,200°K. Colour films are designed to render colours accurately under either of these conditions.
While the human eye and brain make colour corrections automatically, film stocks can only work properly under either one condition or the other. Therefore with daylight, electronic flash and fluorescent light a daylight stock must be used and in tungsten light only a tungsten film will render the generally redder light correctly.

Transparency films
Daylight colour films

The choice offered among colour films to be used in daylight conditions at first seems very much the same as that offered for black and white films — they range from very slow ultra-fine grain to high speed with less

definition. However, the kind of colour quality that you will get with a very fine grain film with a low rating such as Kodachrome II (ASA 25) will differ from even a closely related film only slightly faster, such as Kodachrome X (ASA 64). A comparison of transparencies from these two films will reveal that they are both capable of producing very fine detail (the edge naturally being with the slower, Kodachrome II), but the colour balance with the faster film is different. Under low lighting, in open shade, for example, Kodachrome X has a more pronounced greenish tinge than Kodachrome II. If you now compare Kodachrome X with another film which is also a daylight transparency film with an ASA rating of 64, such as Kodak's Ektachrome X, you will find that skin tones and general colour rendition will be brighter and richer with Ektachrome, but that fine detail will be sharper with the Kodachrome. Other factors must also be considered in your choice of film. For instance, Ektachrome film can be developed by many different colour laboratories around the world, or in a properly equipped home darkroom. Kodachrome, however, can *only* be processed by a Kodak laboratory. Another 'plus' factor for Ektachrome is its ability to be 'pushed' in the developing process. Most colour laboratories will process this film at a higher ASA rating—a two stop increase to 250 ASA being considered a safe limit, beyond which colour balance and image quality deteriorate severely. High speed daylight transparency films are also available, from High Speed Ektachrome (ASA 160) to GAF 500 (ASA 500, formerly known as Anscochrome 500). The latter film is particularly good with its combination of ultra high speed, sharp detail and a full range of well-balanced colours with good whites and skin tones.

Artificial light films

When working under a wide variety of different tungsten filament lighting conditions, many professional photographers use High Speed Ektachrome Type B (ASA 125). This is a very versatile film which works well under differing conditions. Ideally, it is recommended for use under tungsten lights with a basic standard colour temperature of 3,200° Kelvin. Check studio lights, such as flood lights and quartz iodine lamps, for their rating. If your lamps have a colour

temperature rating of 3,400° Kelvin, a Type A colour film should be used for perfect colour balance.
For shooting in available light however, you may use the film under less than perfect conditions if you are prepared to accept unusual colour balances. For example, normal household bulbs tend to be yellowish and will give an orange cast.
When working with fluorescent lighting, use daylight colour films rather than tungsten balance films. The correct gelatin to use to correct colour perfectly is given in the section on Filters.

Making the choice

With so many factors to consider, choosing the right colour film becomes a very subjective experience. It will depend essentially on: the general colour quality wanted (e.g. Kodachrome for more subtle colour, Ektachrome for brighter colours under a wider range of conditions); the quality of skin tones given by a film; the definition wanted (a fast or slow film); the type of lights you will be working with (tungsten, daylight); and how much light there will be to work with. Finally, you must consider whether you want to have special processing (i.e. from a colour laboratory) or whether it matters that the film can only be processed by the manufacturer (as with Kodachrome films).

Negative colour films

If you are primarily interested in a colour print for your final picture, a wide variety of negative colour films are also available. It is usual for them to have an ASA rating of 80 and most laboratories throughout the world can handle processing. This film type offers the additional advantage of being suitable to use for making black and white enlargements, provided that you use the correct paper, such as Kodak Panalure. Furthermore, colour transparencies can easily be obtained from the colour negatives. This last feature may be useful if you want to reproduce a photograph for a magazine, as they usually prefer to work with transparency originals.
High quality colour prints in a reasonably large size, 8 inches x 10 inches, are generally quite expensive, as are colour prints which are made up from transparency films. The cost of the latter is mainly due to the necessity of making an inter-negative before making a print.

What Do You Want to Achieve

The precise qualities which make a photograph artistic, or erotic, or both are not always immediately identifiable.

Simple figure studies which isolate the body and concentrate on form and composition will usually satisfy the most basic aesthetic considerations. Eroticism is a quality a bit more difficult to define. It combines a split-second emotional insight with subtle, sensitive lighting. Prying camera work or grotesque postures are not conducive to an erotic photograph. The key to capturing a quality of eroticism is probably to stir the imagination, to suggest rather than display. Qualities which suggest vulnerability or evoke memories and excite sensual perceptions such as touch or smell all contribute to the erotic in a photograph. A peculiar slant of the head or a fleeting expression may mean the difference between a perfectly ordinary picture and a memorable one.

A photographer's choice of model will depend largely upon what he is trying to accomplish. Is the desired effect moody, mysterious, glamorous, very natural-looking, or even humorous? In the picture at the right, for instance, the warm brown of the model's body is crucial to the effect which has been achieved on the pine background. A very pale skin tone would not have communicated the same feeling. This picture was taken with a Nikon F camera and a 50 mm f2 lens. The film was Kodachrome II, daylight and electronic flash was used with lights bounced into a silver umbrella. Exposure time was 60th second at f8. At the left, a simple figure study which concentrates on form and tonal qualities. It was shot with a Nikon F camera and a 105mm lens. The film was Kodak FX 135 rated at 80 ASA for more contrast on the negative. The exposure time was 60th second at f8-f11 with electronic flash.

MALCOLM SCOULAR

Alphabet of Terms

Aperture A circular hole of varying diameter which controls the amount of light entering a camera lens. On most cameras, markings known as f-numbers indicate the measure of light passing through the lens. The smaller the f number, the larger the lens opening. F numbers are calculated in such a way that each number represents twice as much as the previous one. For example, f2 lets in twice the amount of light as f2.8. The exposure time of a picture will be related to the size of the aperture.

ASA The abbreviation for the American Standards Association, which set standard arithmetical speed ratings for film manufacturers. This term indicates the maximum speed (or the film's sensitivity to light) which the manufacturer calculates under ideal conditions.
The film rated at 125 ASA is twice as sensitive to light as one rated at 64 ASA. Again, the speed of a film will affect the exposure time.

Centre-weighted A term referring to a through-the-lens light meter which takes the main reading from light which comes from the central area of the picture.

Colour temperature In simple terms this measure refers to the heat given off by a theoretical perfect light source. It is measured in degrees Kelvin (°K). Colour films are specially balanced for use under light of different colour temperatures—i.e. daylight, 6000°K, or tungsten, 3200°K.

Depth of field The distance between the nearest and farthest parts of the subject which can be focused acceptably on a common plane.

Focal length The distance from the optical centre of the lens to the plane of the film, when the lens is focused at infinity. The longer the focal length, the greater the magnification of the image. For example, in 35mm cameras, a 28mm lens is a wide angle and a 135mm lens is a telephoto.

Focusing magnifier A device used in making photographic prints. It magnifies the grain pattern of a negative in the enlarger and makes focusing of the positive image on the print much easier.

Grain The grain size distribution on the film emulsion will largely determine the amount of contrast (i.e. the range of grey tones) a film can produce. Most high contrast films are fine-grained and slow; low-contrast ones are generally coarse-grained and faster.

Guide numbers These are simply numerical factors which enable a person using flash lighting to calculate the correct lens opening to use with a particular speed film.

Image brightness Basically, the amount of light given off by the image being photographed. The same subject can be imaged at various levels of brightness with different lenses. The aperture and the distance between the lens and the image affect image brightness.

Internegative When a high quality colour print is wanted and the original picture was taken on transparency film, it will be necessary to copy the transparency on to an internegative film and make the colour print from this.

Line conversion A method of printing high contrast black-and-white negatives which reduces continuous grey tones to powerful graphic black and white lines.

Paper grades Paper used for printing black and white photographs usually is referred to by numbers which indicate grades of contrast; 2 is normal, 3 is hard and 4 is very hard.

Parallax The error which occurs in the picture area when the viewfinder on the camera is positioned at a slightly different angle than the taking lens, as in the twin-lens reflex and the coupled rangefinder.

Safelights These are used in darkrooms. They consist of a filter placed over a light bulb which prevents photographic paper from being overexposed (i.e. fogging).

Slave unit An electronic device which will automatically fire additional flash units simultaneously.

Tungsten This refers to the element used for the filaments of photoflood lamps and household light bulbs. When working with colour films, you must use a type which has been specifically designed to produce good colour quality under these lighting conditions.

The romantic quality captured (right) was achieved by breathing on the lens when shooting and by semi-solarizing at the print stage.

KIM SAYER

Working with Models

Finding and choosing a model is usually something of a problem for the amateur photographer. If the decision to take photographs is prompted by inspiration from a particularly beautiful or exceptional looking woman, the only problem remaining is to ask her permission. It's always helpful if you can offer to pay a nominal fee, for goodwill, but you should at least give the model free prints from the session and pay any incidental costs, such as fares and meals.

Usually, there are no problems in booking a professional model from one of the recognized agencies which exist in most large cities. Fairly exact details of the session must be given and, of course, the model can refuse an assignment. For the amateur photographer, the thought of one hour's photography with a professional model at considerable cost per hour may be daunting. If you intend to sell the photographs, then the model fees may be justified, provided that you are sufficiently experienced.

Another source of photographic subjects is through life classes at a local art school. Rates at these schools are usually lower than at professional modelling agencies, and many of the models are willing to take on extra work for outside photographers and artists. These models often provide a wider variety in age and physical build than the conventional model agencies. Finally, do not overlook friends and relations. They may be very helpful, especially if you feel at all embarrassed or awkward to begin with. However, when working with amateur models, one attitude you are apt to encounter is characterized in the declaration, 'Oh, but I'm not at all photogenic'. The answer to such a response is that, obviously, some people are extremely photogenic, which is why they make their living as models; but anyone can be photographed well if approached sensitively and honestly. Sometimes the most naive, gauche

JOHN GARRETT

amateur model may have a rare
natural quality which a professional
model will never achieve in a lifetime.
Your choice of model depends on what
you are trying to accomplish, Do you
want to take a humorous picture, an
artistic study of the human form, an
erotic photograph, or a straight pin-
up picture? Usually your best choice
will be a model who is relatively
young, on the slim side or at least
well-proportioned (the camera has a
tendency to exaggerate plumpness and
the kind of hollows and folds that
come with age), and with a face and
character you find interesting. It
is unimportant to look for a typically
attractive sexual archetype, as this
may immediately give your picture a
stereotyped look.

How to direct the model

The relationship between the photographer and the subject is of primary
importance. Learning how to direct
your subject to achieve precisely what
you are looking for and learning when
to let the subject simply be herself
will be vital to your development as a
photographer.

Experience in photographing nude
subjects produces at least two general
guidelines. First, you must explain,
as clearly and eloquently as possible,
the general results you are looking for.
Secondly, you must make it
clear that your primary interest
in the subject is for photographic
purposes. If you feel nervous, as you
may do in your first few endeavours,
an informal talk with the model
beforehand may clear the air and
should definitely help her to know
what you're trying to achieve.
Before starting to take pictures,
prepare everything you will be
needing for your various techniques
so that there is no need to fumble
unnecessarily. Also—think ahead
about your model's comfort. Is the
room a pleasant temperature? Is there
a comfortable chair with a few
cushions to support her back if
necessary?

Start with something simple that
helps the model to relax. Ask her to
adopt an attitude of repose. Often
the positions which people find most
comfortable are very beautiful.

*Choice of model is important to the
final effect of a photograph. The
model, left, would be appropriate to
use for a subdued, introspective figure-
study, while the model on the right,
would be suitable for a more glamorous
approach.*

JEAN-PIERRE BOURGEOISE

21

Be prepared to accept a pose which is at least close to what you are looking for, and if you notice that this attitude is transient and going to change very quickly, ask the model to stay exactly as she is for a minute or two. Then capture the look as quickly as possible. While the model adopts various poses, observe as much as you can about the subject. Bodies often look very different unclothed from clothed. Take careful visual stock of everything—how the person moves, the proportions of the body, attitudes that come naturally to the subject, any unusual marks which you may want to omit in your photographs. Even more important than these mechanical details, however, is to look at your subject with a fresh eye. What kind of person is she, is it better to leave her to respond in her own way to the setting in which she finds herself, or should you expect her to confront you? Do you want the subject to respond directly to your eyes?

Pat formulas for directing models are not very helpful, since the most important factor is that each subject will be completely different and you may feel differently towards her from one day to the next. The real challenge lies in creating a rapport with the subject which will allow you to create a photograph together. With all models it is important to give frequent encouragement and to make the model aware of your confidence in her.

Whenever you are working on difficult poses or for long periods of time stop at regular intervals for a break. Aside from giving the subject a needed rest, you will give yourself a chance to get new ideas flowing and to discuss them thoroughly with the model.

Music can be a help or a hindrance in creating moods. If your subject has an understanding and feeling for musical movement and this is part of the result you are looking for, then appropriate music can be invaluable.

A relaxed model, who understands the photographer's objectives, will usually be easy to direct. On the left, the model is unposed and in a reflective mood. On the right, the models were required to project a particular quality. Above and far right, the models were specially posed and gaze directly at the camera. Left, the model was required to look away from the camera and hold a carefully balanced pose.

MICHAEL BOYS

PIRAN MURPHY

The Natural Nude

Familiar indoor settings

One advantage of indoor work is that you have the opportunity of photographing your subject as an integral part of the surroundings. Many photographers find it natural to work with a subject in a room which reflects her tastes and personality. A bedroom, for instance, is a place where people usually surround themselves with very personal belongings. But any room has possibilities which can be used to create an interesting atmosphere— living areas, bathrooms, balconies, even games rooms and children's rooms. Do not feel inhibited by the ordinary

— use your imagination to think up unusual approaches to everyday situations.

Lighting

If there is good natural light, there is no reason to disturb the setting with cumbersome lighting equipment, and flash is apt to be unpredictable. Natural light normally produces life-like results and many top photographers prefer to use it. If the level of light in a room is a little low, you might try replacing the natural light with light bulbs of twice the normal wattage (i.e. perhaps 150-200 watts), or use standard

photoflood bulbs. This technique has the effect of providing 100 per cent more light in a room without essentially changing the natural quality of the room's lighting.

Things to look for

Allow the model to feel completely at ease and try to make yourself as inconspicuous as possible. Let her move about freely and be ready to capture any inspiring moments. One thing to keep in mind when you are shooting is the exciting visual incongruity between the human form and certain inanimate objects. Remember, too, there's also the

element of surprise—seeing someone doing an everyday job like writing a letter in the nude.
Try analyzing the human form in terms of shape—for instance, look for the contrasts and complements in furniture shapes. Investigate the

Many professional photographers prefer to work in daylight with natural settings, despite the difficulties often encountered with lighting conditions or the weather. The three photographs shown here were taken in simple indoor settings and lit to emphasize warm skin tones.

SALLY PATCH

INCZEDY-GOMBOS/TRANSWORLD

effects of different colours and textures for backgrounds. Spatial relationships are still another facet to explore in indoor settings; what happens to the body when backed into a corner, when left alone in a completely bare room? Try to take photographs by a window. There are few things that look as lovely as the light from a window softly bathing the contours of a nude form standing nearby. Or shoot looking in through a window from outside, as though to frame the girl's isolation.

Choosing an outdoor location

The nude and nature are ideal partners for photographic studies. Choosing a location is always complicated by the need for privacy and the weather. Look for the different possibilities in various types of

Left above, this photograph (shot with a Pentax, single-lens reflex camera, 35mm lens on Ektachrome X film 60th second at f5.6) successfully captures a feeling of quiet and solitude. Left below, a late afternoon shot of a nude girl sitting in a large, nearly empty room depicts the usual as unusual. Right above, a cool refreshing atmosphere has been captured in this picture, taken with a Nikon F camera on Kodachrome II 60th second at f5.6. The lens was a 105mm with a 1A and a 10 magenta filter. Below, note the contrast between the picture at the left using portable electronic flash (30th second at f11) and the one at the right without flash (60th second at f8). They were both taken on a Mamiya C3 camera (twin lens reflex) with a 50mm lens, on Ektachrome X film.

SPIKE POWELL

M. de St. OUEN

settings. In a forest, the masses of the trees can make a beautiful confining surround; in an open field, the model becomes a free figure in a natural space; by the sea there is the movement of sand and water. But there are literally dozens of other possible outdoor locations to choose from — mountains, cliffs, moors, marsh lands, sand dunes, orchards, lakes. Each one has a different character which can be used to heighten a particular mood or to help you to formulate unusual compositions — gnarled trees, sky and clouds.

Light and weather conditions

Do not feel that you must have beautifully clear, sunny days for outdoor photography. Dull, overcast days are excellent for obtaining soft, subtle colours. Light situations can vary widely — dappled shade in the forest, clouds and open sky in fields, brilliantly harsh light by the sea. To be prepared for changing conditions, take along a variety of film stocks. (See the section on choosing the right film for more details.)

Likewise, do not be deterred by cold weather. Plan your shots thoroughly and select the exact location beforehand. Have the model dress in warm clothing which is easy to remove (a cloak is ideal). Avoid restrictive clothing as this may leave unsightly marks on the body which disappear slowly in cold weather.

Unusual settings

You can conjure up new moods by photographing in completely incongruous settings—a derelict house for example. This type of situation offers opportunities to make powerful visual comments about the relationship people have with a house; dereliction somehow never quite destroys the evidence of people.

You might treat your nude subject as an intruder into the old house, who gradually becomes involved in what the house must have been like when it was inhabited.

Any place which has some sort of definite atmosphere makes an imaginative setting — look for lovely old barns, attics, stairways, doorways. You are limited only by your imagination and the subject's spirit of adventure.

The nude form offers innumerable opportunities for experimentation in natural outdoor settings, as shown in these photographs.

MICHAEL BOYS

Working in the Studio

Working in the studio gives the photographer two main advantages: he will have absolute control over lighting, and he will be able to isolate the subject from any surround and treat it as a separate entity. The studio set-up gives the photographer flexibility to portray the subject in any way that he chooses.

The eight lighting set-ups described on this page are intended as a basic guide from which to begin. You will soon discover variations which suit the effects you particularly want.

1 The classic 'three-quarter' lighting situation. Begin by arranging a floodlamp at the level of the model's face. Then raise and lower it for variations.

2 Three-quarter light used again, but turned away from the subject and bounced into an umbrella reflector. The effect will be to widen the angle of the light and soften its quality.

3 To isolate the subject from the surroundings and leave a white background behind her, shine a wide beam of light from a diffused floodlamp through the background and combine it with a diffuse three-quarter light.

4 To achieve a silhouette effect with some tonal quality try bouncing one light from the background and move it around to get the precise desired effect.

5 Two diffused floodlamps, each set at a 45° angle, will provide an even, gentle light. To futher accentuate light and shade, one light may be moved further away from the subject.

6 For soft, all-over lighting on a reclining nude (seamless, paper ground) bounce light from a single floodlamp above the subject, again moving the light for the precise effect wanted.

7 To emphasize the modelling on limbs and shoulders and highlight the hair, use a spotlamp for the main illumination, and a floodlamp behind the subject. Fill in deep shadows with another floodlamp in the front area.

8 A strong floodlamp behind the model will produce a brilliant outline or halo effect around the subject's body.

Left, a typical photographic studio with a session in progress. See the interview with Malcolm Scoular for further details.

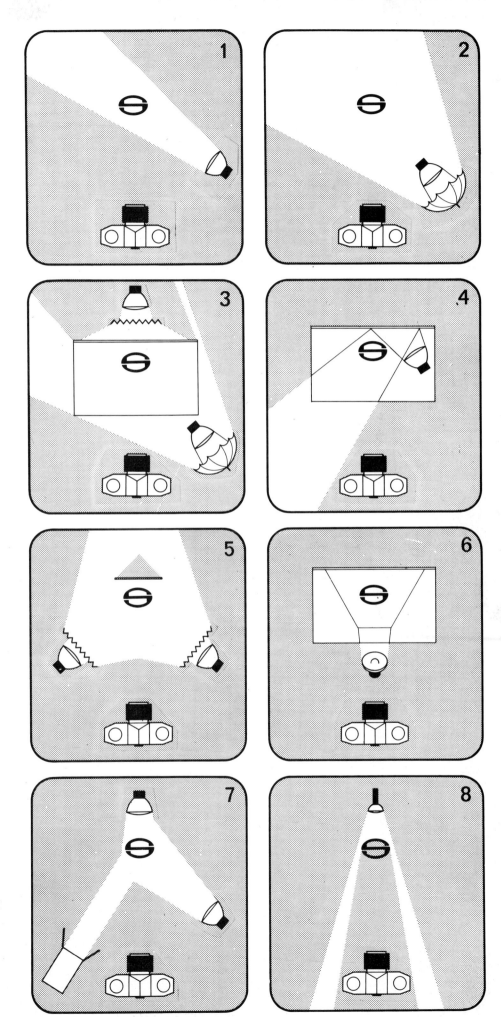

Backgrounds

One of the simplest ways to isolate the subject is to use a plain, seamless paper background usually known as 'Colorama'. Rolls of this fairly heavy-weight paper come in various widths, normally ranging from 9 feet to 12 feet in lengths of 36 feet. A very wide selection of colours is available including white. When working with Colorama, you will often find that you want to extend the roll down over the floor and pose the model on the paper. Be certain not to walk on the paper when wearing shoes and do not place objects on it which will leave marks. With careful use, a roll of Colorama can be used many times over and is a good investment for a studio.

Other backgrounds can of course be used. Fabric of almost any type can make a suitable background or surround. Frequently the texture and general look of a fabric will be influential in determining the atmosphere of the final picture. Consider hessian, PVC and other vinyls, fur, leather, lace, silk, velvet and satin. Each type of fabric will to some extent affect the light conditions of the picture. A shiny PVC material will bounce light off the body, while velvet will tend to absorb light, and give generally subtler effects. If you are working with 'flats' — large, flat backboards — which must be covered with fabric, be certain to eliminate all wrinkles or marks so that the final pictures are not marred by them.

Props

If you wish to emphasize a particular aspect of the body or to create an atmosphere in which the nude form plays a part, props of some sort are vital.

Here again imagination and a clear sense of what it is you are trying to achieve will determine the props that you use. For example, rings, bracelets and necklaces can be particularly effective for enhancing shapes and lending a bit of colour to otherwise uniform skin tones.

Apart from props other techniques may be used to create special looks — greasing the model's body with oil, for instance, will make it look smooth and shimmering. Baby oil or even vaseline can be used.

Types of lighting

In studio work part of the challenge in taking good pictures is to combine all the technical know-how with some visual imagination. The tone of the pictures you want to take will to some extent suggest the colour and type of background you will use, whether or not you use props and the type of lighting you will need. Basically, there are three types of artificial light to choose from: the spotlight for hard lighting (i.e. bright with deep shadows); the flood light which is also hard but can be adjusted to softer light at greater distances; the diffused flood or reflected light which is essentially soft.

Lighting equipment you will need

A wide variety of different lighting equipment is, of course, available. The types discussed here offer a very good basic range to work with. A spot lamp which can be adjusted to give a narrow, bright beam or a wider, softer one, is the most usual for basic 'hard' lighting. Photoflood lamps, corrected exactly for use with colour film, sometimes come with built-in reflectors, and otherwise must be used with lighting stands.

If you want to have a gentler light for softer modelling of the nude form, you may prefer to diffuse the photoflood light, either by placing some opalescent glass or tracing paper in front of the bulb, or by 'bouncing' the light into an umbrella reflector or off a sheet of white card. The latter will spread the angle of the beam of light and also give it a much softer quality.

Electronic flash as a method of lighting is no longer the exclusive tool of the professional photographer. There are many powerful, very small units now available, all of which are balanced for daylight colour film. A 'slave unit' is also a good piece of equipment to have if you will be working with more than one flash gun. These clever little devices automatically trigger off additional flash units at the appropriate times to complete your lighting arrangement.

For the beginner the major limitation with flash in the studio is that it will take considerable experience to gauge the exact effect produced by the angle of direct or 'bounced' flash light. With other types of lighting systems it is easy to move the lights about until you actually see the effect that you want. The latest advance in lighting equipment is the quartz-iodine lamp, which is generally quite small and delivers an astonishing light output for its size. The disadvantage of these lights are their fragile nature and the high cost of bulb replacements. QI lighting stands are available which are much smaller than photoflood stands and are equipped with little 'barn doors' which can regulate the overall angle of the light.

When working with a collection of various different lights a colour temperature meter, such as the Sixticolour, is useful. This will indicate whether or not lights have fallen below the standard colour temperature of 3200° Kelvin — the temperature under which most tungsten colour films are to be used. (See the section on colour films.) In addition, a light meter will usually be required (see the section on cameras and equipment) to calculate exact exposures.

Placing the lights

In general, the fewer number of lights used the better the effect; over-lighting has spoiled many potentially good pictures. The primary or modelling light is the central one, and if it produces the desired effect on its own, do not complicate the set-up with other lights. If you want some detail in the shadows, reflect some light off a piece of white paper. In addition to the primary light, a secondary light can be used for an overall shadowless picture. A 'back light' directly behind the subject can be used to highlight hair and other features. Examples of different lighting set-ups are shown in the diagrams.

Posing the model

Ideas for poses can be found by studying the work of different photographers. However, the model herself will dictate to a certain extent the type of pose. If she has an oval face and good features for instance, then a full-face pose may be excellent. Try to choose the best features and accentuate these, while minimizing those which are less flattering or which do not suit the type of picture you want to take.

Studio work offers the opportunity to control the situation by artificial means. Right, the girl's body was oiled with vaseline and water was poured over her from above. Inset, distinctive textures can enhance skin tones.

JEAN-PIERRE BOURGEOISE

MICHAEL JAMES WARD

Picture Compositions

CAROLINE ARBER

SPIKE POWELL

PIRAN MURPHY

Basic geometric shapes and their relationships on overlapping planes are the foundation of picture composition. The normal mechanics of visual design apply to photography.
In the pictures shown on this page and opposite, simple shapes, i.e. triangles, ovals, parallel lines and diagonals form the basis of the central picture areas.

Picture composition is a matter of visual judgement. So-called rules can only provide a guide for the photographer; they should never be used as absolutes. There is a countless variety of subjects and picture demands which the photographer must resolve according to his own visual sense.

Basic design considerations will provide the best guide for arranging the subject within the picture frame. Parallel, vertical or horizontal lines within the picture format suggest stability and uniformity. Pictures which are arranged around steeply converging or diverging angular lines will suggest action. Balance and symmetry may be important to the effect of some pictures, but beware of creating boring designs. A lone subject placed dead centre in the picture frame is the sort of arrangement that can look very dull. This is equally true of many strictly formal arrangements. As with any visual art, continual experience will alter and help develop a photographer's sense of composition and design.

Picture composition need not always be perfectly symmetrical. Carefully contrived balance can look artificial or simply boring. Some of the most effective photographs are those which appear to capture and hold a particular moment quite still for careful investigation. The eye accepts much which is not geometrically balanced, if other qualities—colour, texture, pattern —contribute something critical to the picture. Back lighting, as seen in the photograph here, emphasizes the sculptural quality of the nude form by producing an outline around the body.

MICHAEL JAMES WARD

35

Left, curves are the central interest in this unusual photograph. Notice how the shape of the body in the picture here breaks the rectangle into triangular areas.

JOHN GARRETT

37

Body Shapes

Visual interpretation of the human form, whether in art or photography, has a long and fascinating tradition. Body shapes alter in appearance as lighting and angle of vision alter. When combined with the infinite variety of body shapes which exist, the opportunity for creating imaginative pictures seems almost limitless.

The nude form offers endless permutations on a single theme, and the opportunities for experimenting with shape, as shape alone, should not be overlooked. Control of lighting will produce either angular or rounded variations of a single feature. For example, the pictures on these pages show a variety of body shapes, taken at different times with different equipment for different purposes.

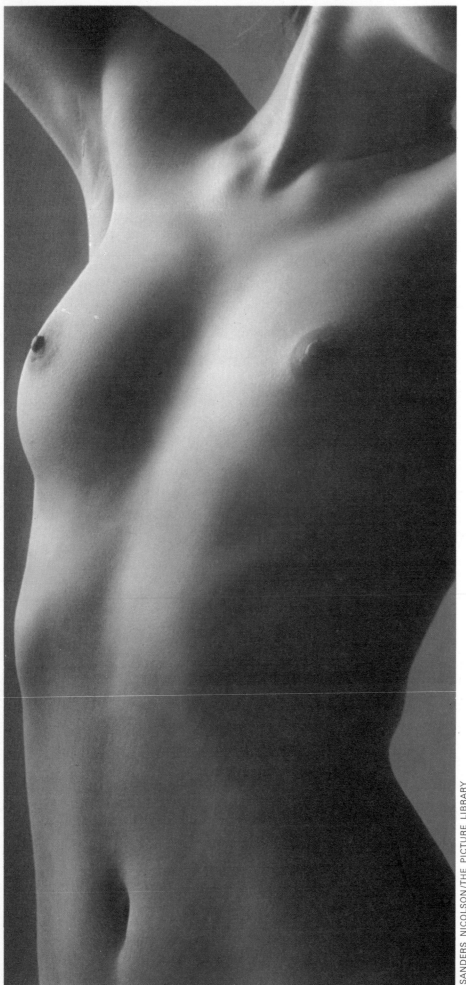

Left, this simple yet evocative shot of a woman's torso was taken with a Hasselblad camera, 150mm lens, on Ektachrome Professional film (50 ASA). A Softar No. 1 filter and an 05 magenta filter were used with electronic flash at an aperture of f16.

Single frames mounted together in some pattern, as with the stacked effect shown right, can make very effective photo-montages. These pictures were taken on a Nikon F camera with a series of lenses. From top to bottom they were a 135mm, a 55mm, and for the final two, a 28mm. A 10 magenta filter was used and the film was Kodachrome II. Bounced light and reflectors were employed.

The photograph at the far right makes use of a single piece of jewelry to bring the body shapes together for maximum impact. Jewelry is often a useful device for accentuating skin texture and colour.

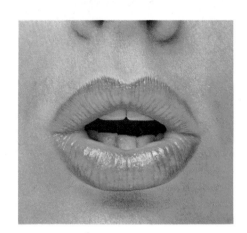

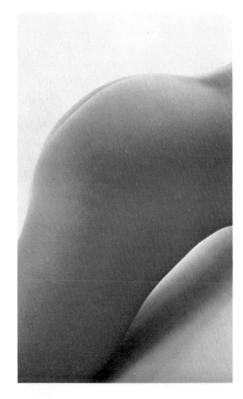

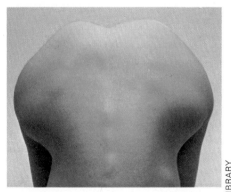

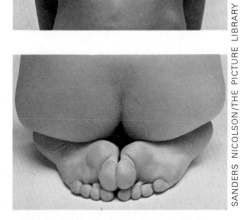

Lighting and Moods

The essence of a good photograph is not to be found in mere technical capabilities. Cameras, lenses, films and the finest mastery of this equipment will not produce an aesthetically pleasing picture unless the photographer has also mastered the complicated relationship between form and light. This sensitive relationship cannot be confined to a strict set of rules or formulas. Some photographers, both amateur and professional, forget that these guides (such as those shown in the section on studio work) are only meant to serve as a basic frame-work for lighting techniques. They should not restrict the creative vision of the photographer or prevent him from trying out unusual approaches.

Above, capture a hint of movement with a slow exposure time.

Light is one of the principle factors in determining the mood of a picture. Decide first what your lighting is meant to emphasize, or minimize. Do you want to present an overall uniform effect, with maximum detail and some loss of three-dimensional qualities? Do you want the subject to stand out from the background? Should the subject be subordinate to the lighting itself, or should the lighting emphasize a specific quality, such as shape, texture, or pattern? Are you attempting to create a gloomy, mysterious mood or a vibrant, exciting one? The answers will determine the lighting which you deploy.

Probably more than any other single factor, lighting can create or destroy a mood or atmosphere which a photographer wants to bring out in his picture.
The top picture was taken with the aid of a tripod in fading sunlight at early evening, hence the strong shadows. The camera used was a Nikon F with a 50mm lens, and the film was Kodachrome II. Exposure was 30th at f4. Above is an unusual effect obtained by bouncing the light from the red bulb into a mirror which reflects on the model's face. The camera was a Nikon F with a 50 mm lens. Exposure was 30th at f1.4 on Kodachrome II. Still another effect, in the picture at the right, is a strong silhouette. In this instance notice how the 'flat' quality of the sky acts very much as a flat backdrop would in a studio setting.

Light patterns are yet another variation which, when introduced into the composition of a photograph, can create a visual impact all their own or enhance and emphasize an existing shape or feature.

Left and right are two excellent examples of the kind of effect which can be achieved by the use of controlled patterns of light. In both instances it is the light streaming in through a window which glances upon and brings to life the form standing in semi-darkness within. Such photographs are heavily dependent upon the sensitivity and acuteness of the photographer's observation. For more information concerning the picture at the right, see the interview with Caroline Arber.

By making deliberate use of the maze of brambles to create a patterned effect on the model's face and body, above, the photographer has cleverly turned a possible disadvantage to positive effect.

42

43

Creative Camera Control

Filters for black and white photography

Filters have essentially two functions in photography. The first is practical — they protect lenses from damage by scratches, thumb prints and moisture. The second is more creative — they change the quality of the light reaching the film emulsion.

In black and white photography filters modify the tones of grey which represent the colours of the original scene. By eliminating selected sections of the colour spectrum normally reaching the film, filters can, for instance, darken the sky, intensify skin tone so that the subject appears tanned, or reduce the haze in distant scenes.

Naturally if you remove part of the light which would normally reach the film, it is necessary to increase the exposure to compensate. The degree of compensation for any given filter is sometimes given as the 'filter factor'. A filter factor of *two* means that you must let in *twice* as much light as you would for a normal exposure (an increase of *one* f-stop). If your camera has through-the-lens metering, however, filter factors may be ignored as the measured light falling on the meter has already passed through the filter and the reading will be adjusted accordingly. If you are photographing an outdoor scene in which you would like the clouds at the back to billow and dominate, then a medium yellow filter will darken the sky and give the edges of the clouds greater contrast. Exposure should be increased by one f-stop.

Indoors, if you feel the subject's body will reproduce very pale on a black and white print, a light green filter will darken the skin tone slightly. In this case exposure should be increased by 2 stops.

Filters for colour photography

When photographing in colour it is much easier to gauge the effect the filter will produce, because you will see through the filter an approximation of the effect reproduced on the film. In general colour photography the two most commonly used filters are the ultra-violet (UV), which will effectively cut down any haze which appears in distant scenes, and the pink skylight filter, which in addition to reducing haze, makes skin tones look slightly warmer and so is very useful in photographing nudes. This skylight filter is particularly useful when working inside with daylight coming into a room, and outside in subdued shade. Most photographers tend to leave this filter on at all times and only replace it with an ultra-violet filter when the scene being photographed demands considerable correction for the blue ultra-violet light rays.

Filters for colour compensation in existing lighting situations

To avoid great expense in buying filters, you can use the very inexpensive Wratten gelatin filters made by Kodak. These come in a wide range of colours and effects. They are supplied square, but come with an overlay containing a series of printed circles so that you can easily cut them to the size of your lens. These filters are inserted between your normal filter (UV or skylight) and the front element of the lens.

The major drawback to these filters is that they are coated with gelatin and scratch very easily. When excessively marked they should be replaced to avoid unnecessary softening or blurring of the image. Gelatin filters can be chosen to help with nearly every situation, thanks to their low cost. For instance, if working near a fluorescent light, you may find a strong green cast will be thrown on the picture area. A 30cc Magenta filter will eliminate this effect. Experiment with filters, however, as light sources can vary enormously. Below is a list of useful filters for both black and white and colour work.

Useful filters for black and white

(The filter numbers are Kodak reference numbers)

8 Yellow: corrects colours to show outdoor scenes in accurate tonal balance (emphasizes cloud details).

52 Light-green: darker skin tones indoors, natural tones outdoors.

25 Red: absorbs ultra-violet rays and strongly accents clouds.

ND Neutral density filter: simply cuts down the amount of light reaching film without affecting its colour. Ideal for outdoor situations where you want to shoot at full aperture, or use a very slow shutter speed in bright light. It is available in various strengths.

Useful filters for colour

(The filter numbers are Kodak reference numbers)

1A Very faint pink: skylight filter, absorbs ultra-violet rays and reduces blue cast caused by aerial haze. Warms skin tones.

2B Very faint yellow: haze filter, absorbs strong ultra-violet rays.

Magenta 30 Pale pink: absorbs green cast from fluorescent light sources.

80B Bluish: converts daylight colour film for use with photoflood lights.

85B Amber: converts Type B colour film for daylight use.

Special effects filters

The polarizing filter is also very useful, ideal for both black and white and colour because it eliminates reflection, and can subtly darken skies and skin tones.

A variety of special filters are also available which will produce any number of different effects — from simple soft-focus to radiating star-like patterns. If you use any of these filters, do so judiciously. Some of the most bizarre ones, such as the multi-faceted prism filter which produces several images from one, can look very cliched unless used imaginatively.

Further creative controls

The list of possible effects and 'tricks of the trade' can be quite extensive and only a few are mentioned here. Zoom lenses, for example, can be used to explode a picture or extension rings are useful devices for close-up work. To degrade the image and achieve a 'soft focus' appearance try placing a sheer stocking over the lens or smearing just a bit of vaseline over the protective filter covering the lens. With a single lens reflex camera you can breathe very gently on the lens to 'mist it over'. Then quickly watch as the mist disappears and take the picture precisely where you want to create a hazy look.

All the photographs on this page
were shot on Ektachrome X film, and
coloured cellophane was held over the
lens (50mm f2). Lighting was natural
daylight and a tripod used for all
pictures. Below, pink, magenta and
mauve cellophane in order from top to
bottom.

In the top picture, below, the unusual
effect was achieved by shooting
through a tube of pink cellophane
held around the lens. A loosely
woven tissue was then passed in front.
Below, blue cellophane and natural
daylight (60th second at f5.6).

The top picture, above, was shot
through a tube of clear cellophane
which was held around the outer rim
of the lens. Green and yellow strips
of cellophane held across the lens
were used for the next two pictures.

Processing

Colour laboratories

Your local colour-processing laboratory can do much more than just develop a roll of colour film. If you are using a film which does not have to be developed exclusively by the manufacturers, an independent laboratory can offer a wide variety of techniques to help you.

One of the most common requests made to laboratories is to 'force' the processing to compensate for the film having been exposed at a higher ASA rating than it was made for. Sometimes, when working in poor lighting conditions a photographer will expose a film at a higher ASA rating rather than use the necessary slower shutter speed. At such times he should tell the laboratory he has 'pushed' the film and by how many stops. The laboratory will then 'force' the processing one or two stops, by increasing the time of the first development, to allow the latent image on the underexposed emulsion to emerge. Some laboratories will charge extra for this service.

If you are worried about the colour balance in your photographs, if you feel, for instance, that the colour will be too blue, you can ask a colour laboratory to correct it. Specialized techniques such as this tend to be done by laboratories which deal mainly with professionals, but they will usually do such work for the serious amateur as well.

Another useful technique which colour laboratories can do is called a 'clip test'. This is a very helpful test if you think your light meter has been reading falsely. The lab will cut a small section from the end of the roll, process this and then adjust the processing for the rest of the roll to compensate for any error of exposure. This test should only be used when you believe that the whole roll has been exposed at the same ASA rating.

Colour laboratories can also compensate for over-exposure of a film by reducing the first development time. This can save film which otherwise would be ruined, and also can act as a creative control when the contrast of the film needs to be reduced for a special effect.

Usually custom laboratories will supply the processed film cut into strips and placed into protective plastic sleeves. If your transparencies require mounting, they will also do this. Mounting, though, is a simple process, and there are so many excellent types of slide mounts available that you might find it better to do this yourself (see the section on framing and mounting).

One final word of caution, custom laboratories will sometimes try to pass off careless work. Do not allow them to do so; make a fuss if they lose your film, scratch the emulsion or mix the film up with someone else's. Beware, too, that when photographing nudes you may encounter unwillingness on the part of some laboratories to process the work, or the pictures may inexplicably get lost.

Colour processing kits

Comprehensive colour processing kits for home developing and printing are now available on the international market. However, despite the inexpensive prints which can be obtained with these kits, there are several drawbacks which should be seriously considered.

First of all to obtain results which are anywhere near accurate, a proper dark room set-up is a must. Next, one of the most difficult requirements to follow with these kits is the need for very precise temperature control of the processing chemicals. On the whole, the procedure is messy, tricky, takes considerable time to prepare and perform, and is not really cheaper than lab-processing. Unless you are especially interested in the processing aspects of photography, you will probably get better results by using a colour laboratory.

Black and white processing
Developers and techniques

Without being drawn into the debate as to whether this developer is better than that, here are three basic processing techniques which will cover all the black and white films and

subjects you are likely to encounter. The first involves a developer which works excellently with a wide variety of films from slow, fine grain to fast emulsions, (see the section on choosing the right film.)

The developer Kodak D76 was first formulated in the 'thirties and has since then given thousands of photographers excellent service. It will make full use of whatever quality the manufacturers have inherently designed in the film, down to very fine grain, and it will also give a long tonal scale. This means that if you are photographing in a situation where there are distinct highlight and shadow areas, the film will record essential information in both areas. When you then come to enlarge from the negative, there will be a smooth transition from the lighter areas to the darker ones. This feature is particularly important in nude photography where the emphasis is on conveying the form of the subject through the use of naturally observed light and shade. Kodak D76 also gives excellent sharpness of detail.

The second technique is to use a developer which has been specifically designed to increase artificially the inherent sensitivity to light (the ASA) that the manufacturers have built into the film. There are a number of these developers on the international market and one of the finest is a British invention, Acuspeed. This is a high-dilution developer which will easily treble the film's recorded ASA rating while retaining surprisingly good quality sharpness and shadow details.

The basic process for the colour solarization shown right involves black and white film. The negative was printed on sheet line film (Ilford N5.51) and separations were made for each colour (4). These were then printed up to size, again on line film, and bleached out until they appeared as clear film. Each bleached film is dyed to the desired colour with waterproof inks.

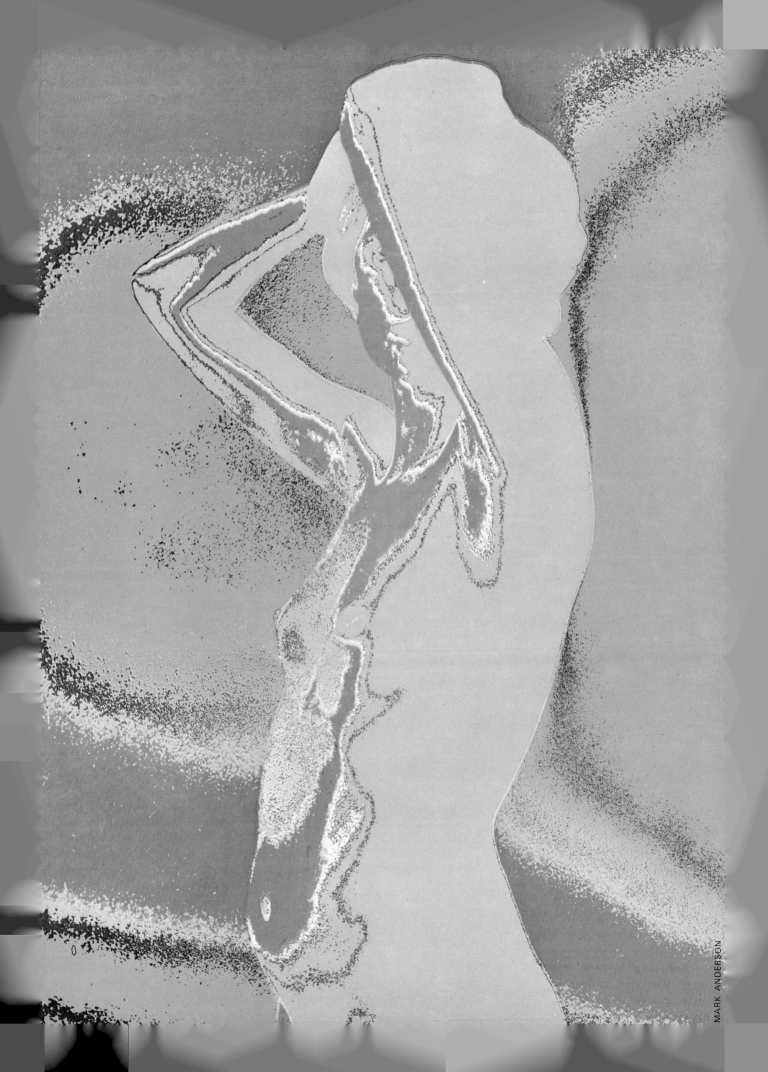

Finally, fine grain developers may be used with any of the very fine grain films, such as Panatomic X. Kodak's Definol is one such developer. It will process a 35mm film, such as Panatomic X, to the equivalent definition negative.

One basic rule should be applied with all processing techniques and that is to achieve the best performance, follow the manufacturer's instructions, but be prepared to make minor adjustments to suit personal requirements.

Processing equipment

A good thermometer 68°F (20°C) is the most usual recommended temperature at which films are to be developed. An accurate, legible thermometer with settings in both Fahrenheit and centigrade scales is essential. Paterson make an excellent one, calibrated in both temperature scales and accurate to $\frac{1}{4}$°F and 0.2°C respectively. It will be more than adequate for your most demanding needs, including colour processing.

A developing tank Stainless steel tanks are preferable to use for their durability, ease of loading and ability to be used and loaded when still wet. However, there are excellent designs available in plastic which are somewhat less expensive than the stainless steel designs.

A timer With any processing, accuracy is important and it is preferable to have a photographic timer on which you can see the time pass at least in quarters of a minute. This is important for timing both overall development, and, with the fine grain developers, agitation during development.

Graduates and mixing containers Now that metrication is nearly world-wide, it is essential to have containers marked in metric units as well as fluid ounces. If you are mixing solutions from powders where large volumes of water are necessary, an ordinary one gallon plastic bucket is perfectly adequate.

Photographic manufacturers make extensive ranges of accurately calibrated transparent plastic containers. These are essential when accurate measurement of developer dilutions are involved. Two particularly useful sizes to have are the 600 ml (about 21 fl. oz.) and the 150 ml (about 5 fl. oz.) for use with high dilution developers.

A plastic funnel This is useful for returning reusable solutions cleanly to their containers.

Plastic gallon containers These are available either through hardware stores, or photographic suppliers. Solution containers can be thoroughly washed and re-used for other solutions. Those with permanently attached tight fitting caps are best.

Film wipers or a chamois cloth Both provide a quick, safe method for removing excess water from the film after completing the washing cycle.

Black cloth changing bag If you do not have a darkroom, a changing bag can be used for loading film into developing tanks. When choosing a changing bag buy one large enough to accommodate a fairly large developing tank in case you should ever need it.

Negative developing chemicals

Developer D76 (or IDII, the Ilford equivalent) for all-purpose fine quality, full emulsion speed processing. Acuspeed (Paterson) for situations requiring artifically high ASA speed. Definol (Kodak) for ultra fine grain.

Stop bath This is usually a 2 per cent solution of glacial acetic acid, which is used to end the action of the developer abruptly, before the film enters the fixer. 'Indicator' stop bath is also available which is yellow in colour when fresh, conveniently turning purple when exhausted after repeated use. Kodak make an Indicator stop bath which comes in a 1 Litre size (35.2 fluid ounces) and, as its working dilution is 1 part ISB to 64 parts water, it will literally last an age.

Fixer A quick acid-hardening fixer should be used to make negatives permanent; 3 minutes fixing time is most usual.

Hypo-eliminator (also known as hypo-clearing agent) This chemical is very low-priced, re-usable (1 ml per gallon will remove the excess hypo from as many as 180 36-exposure black and white films) and essential if you wish your negatives to last indefinitely. Removing the excess hypo in the fixer with this chemical instead of washing after fixing means that washing time will be reduced (5 minutes instead of 30), and the negatives will be of 'archival permanence'. Kodak regard this as a period of 100 years.

Wetting agent This is simply a very concentrated high quality detergent which removes dirt and grit from film surfaces.

Anti-oxidant spray This is useful to prevent chemicals stored in large containers from spoiling.

Step-by-step procedure for professional quality negatives

1. Load the film in total darkness into the developing tank reels.

2. Measure out the correct quantity of developer and bring it to the correct temperature, 68°F (20C). The simplest and most consistent way to use D76 developer is to dilute it 1:1 with water. This increases the development time a little (10 minutes at 68°F, instead of 8 minutes when the developer is used at full strength), but it is more economical.

3. Pour the developer into the tank and set the timer immediately.

4. Rap the developing tank firmly on its base. This will dislodge any air bubbles which may cling to the surface of the film as the developer is poured in, and it will ensure even development.

5. Agitate the film at the intervals specified by the manufacturers throughout the developing time. Some plastic tanks have a provision for inversion agitation as an alternative to using a stirring rod. This ensures that the developer reaches all the area of the film evenly.

6. When development is finished, promptly pour the solution away and immediately replace with the stop bath. Agitate for 15 seconds.

7. Pour the stop bath back into its container (unless exhausted).

8. Pour the rapid fixer in, setting the timer for the recommended time; agitate occasionally.

9. Replace the rapid fixer in its container.

10. Rinse films thoroughly for 2 minutes in running water.

11. Quickly inspect the film to ensure the fixer has done its job. Good negatives should have a full range of greys and should not show great areas of black, which indicates that highlights have been over-developed and 'blocked up'. If the negatives look very evenly transparent or 'thin' either you have allowed insufficient exposure (check your light meter) or insufficient development (check the solution and timer).

12. Pour the hypo-cleaning agent in and agitate normally for two minutes.

13. Replace the hypo-cleaning agent in its container.

14. Wash negatives in running water for about 5 minutes. Remember too much washing can be dangerous as it will soften the emulsion making it vulnerable to scratching.

15. Thoroughly wet a chamois until it is completely soft and pliable. Wring the excess moisture from the leather, fold it around the film, and gently run

the leather down its entire length. Hang the film from a convenient point as you do this.

16. If you are using stainless steel reels, a tip for quick film-drying is to reload the damp films onto the reels and rest them on a dust-free surface. Then place a domestic hairdryer approximately two feet away so the flow of hot air will pass through the reels. The films will dry in 3 to 5 minutes. It is much better to dry them quickly in this way, since hanging them up for any length of time will expose them to dust. However, make sure you do not blow dust all over them with an old hairdryer!

Storing negatives

If you intend to proof rolls of 35mm film on 8x10-inch paper, the complete film can be conveniently cut into strips of five or six negatives and filed in separate strips in a negative envelope. You can place all the negatives in one envelope without damaging them.

Filing may seem to be a problem. But only certain basic information needs to be recorded — and that is the date of processing and the number of the roll processed in that month. These numbers may then be recorded in a processed-negative index book. Each month's negatives should then be filed separately. When making a print from, say, the twelfth roll of January, 1974, the frame number of the actual negative should be added to the roll-file number for completely accurate cross reference. Contact sheets should naturally also be filed in months, numerically. Once you have a system, all that remains is to keep it up to date.

Any black and white negative can be made into a sepia print, left. The negative is processed in the normal way and the print is treated with a special sepia wash.

Working in the Darkroom

Darkroom equipment

It is important that your darkroom divides into two clear areas — a 'dry' bench for your enlarger, paper, negatives and accessories; and a 'wet' bench for processing and washing.

Enlarger If you will be working with small format photographs, use an enlarger with a glassless negative carrier.

A good enlarging lens is essential to have for best results; a poor lens will distort even the best quality negative.

Easel The easel to hold the print paper should be both perfectly square and accurate in distance. It should hold the paper completely flat.

Focusing magnifier This is a great help when focusing the negative on the easel. They are inexpensive and save eyestrain by helping you to focus on the grain of the negative.

Foot switch for the enlarger A device which will leave your hands free to make adjustments.

10 inch x 12 inch x ¼ inch glass plate To hold negatives flat for making contact proofs. A glass plate can do the job just as effectively as a special slotted contact frame.

Print trimmer Necessary for cutting neat uniform print sizes. Check that it is absolutely square.

Thermometer A film processing thermometer will be perfectly adequate.

Graduates See the section on black and white negative processing.

Plastic trays These are for holding prints in the developing solution. Use 12 inch x 10 inch trays for 8 inch x 10 inch prints.

Print tongs To keep your hands dry (very important) and free from irritation from the chemicals.

Safelights Those with inter-changeable filters are particularly useful. With a dark green filter, you can for example, inspect negatives as they are developing.

Print washer These come in many designs and sizes, so you can choose one to suit your needs.

Print dryer A double-sided 11 inch x 14 inch dryer will usually be adequate.

Black and white printing

The first requirement for a good black and white print is a good negative. A good negative will have a full range of grey tones and will approximate as nearly as possible the tonal values present in the original subject.

If you have exposed the film correctly, and developed it to its optimum (avoiding temptation to over-develop slightly 'just to make sure the image is there') the negative should print with ease on a normal grade of paper. With Kodak, for example, this is grade 2. You may find, however, that you prefer to have the slightly fuller range of tones that grade 1 ('soft') paper can give. Hard paper (grade 3 or even 4) may be used to rescue thin negatives. However, although an image will be produced, grey tones are usually sacrificed.

Test strips

To achieve the perfect print, it is always worthwhile to make a test strip of a variety of exposures. To do this place a strip of your chosen paper over the main picture area projected on to the easel by the enlarging lens. Put the enlarger light on, but keep a safelight in position in front of the lens. Using a sheet of black cardboard, expose the paper to the white light. Give the first quarter of the test strip an exposure of, say, 5 seconds. Continue, moving the black cardboard back another quarter of the length of the strip and expose each section for 5 seconds. When you reach the end of the strip, you will have a sheet of paper containing four different exposures for the same negative — i.e. 5, 10, 15 and 20 seconds. Develop this test strip for the time you intend to use for the final print, (usually 90 seconds). It is imperative that the developer is used at the correct temperature (68°F or 20°C) and that all chemicals are fresh and are used at their full working strength. After development, stop bath and fixing, examine the strip under a bright white light. Choose the exposure which gives the tonality and contrast you find most acceptable. The key to good prints is to expose the paper for the minimum time necessary to produce a fully toned print, ranging from rich blacks to delicate greys in the skin tones. As you develop the print on the paper,

watch to see the image come up in the developing solution. If you can see that it will reach the required density long before the ideal developing time of 90 seconds is up, then you have over-exposed the paper and the resultant print will be 'muddy' (turgid shadow areas and dull highlights). Even if you remove the print from the solution before the 90 seconds is up, you cannot cure this muddiness.

Making the final print

After deciding on the best exposure time, you should carefully refocus the negative on the easel and make your exposure.

Process the exposed paper carefully. Using tongs, place the emulsion (shiny, or picture) side face down in the developer, and make sure that the developer immediately covers every part of the paper.

Once development is complete, transfer the print to a fresh solution of stop bath for 5 to 10 seconds, and then to the fixer. Most modern rapid fixers will complete fixing in less than five minutes. After the fixing time has elapsed, transfer the print to a running water rinse for a minute then immerse it for 2 minutes in a hypo clearing agent. Now the print is ready for its final five minutes washing time; once this is done the print will have the advantage of being, like the negative developing process, 'archivally permanent'.

It is always worth examining the print in normal room light before the final washing. This is very important, as appearances under the safelight in the darkroom can be deceptive. If the print is generally satisfactory, but certain areas of the picture seem lighter or darker than they should be, then you may decide to correct this.

Supplementary printing skills

The most common methods of correcting print areas which are too light or too dark are known as 'burning in' and 'dodging'.

'**Burning in**' simply means that after making your basic overall exposure you selectively allow additional light from the enlarging lens to reach areas which you consider should be darker. This is usually done by allowing light to pass through a small hole pierced

through a piece of opaque, black
cardboard.

'**Dodging**' is done using a small piece
of opaque black material attached to
a thin, rigid piece of non-reflecting
wire; by moving this over the paper
you can prevent light from reaching
areas of the picture which your first
print has shown are too dark. It is
most important with these procedures
never to allow the dodger or the
burning-in instrument to remain
stationary, as this will produce a
print on which your corrections can
easily be seen. Keep the instruments
moving so that any corrections will
be indistinguishable from that of a
'straight' print.

Creative controls in the darkroom

Apart from controls which can be
produced by over and under developing
a negative or print, there are numerous
other ways to manipulate photographic
images. For instance, solutions of
ordinary fabric dyes can be used to
produce a whole range of possible
tints. Sepia tints can be made by
using bleach and copper intensifier.
To obtain a grainy effect on a film
which does not have grainy character-
istics, try sandwiching a translucent
backing (such as those in which colour
transparencies are frequently
returned from a laboratory) tightly to
your negative before printing it. The
grain pattern which results from the
enlargement of the plastic texture
can be very interesting.
Soft focus in the darkroom can be
achieved in much the same way it is
with the camera lens; that is by
putting a stocking over the enlarging
lens before exposing the paper.
There are several ways to produce a
line image (all black and white — no
grey tones) from a black and white
negative. One way is to make a print
with very definite areas of contrast,
perhaps on a 'hard' paper, being sure
that the areas of dark tone that
delineate the subject are not lost.
Take a photograph of this print on
the slowest, most fine-grained film
available and deliberately over-expose
it slightly. Develop normally and make
a print on a 'hard' grade paper. If grey
tones still exist take another photograph of this print and make another
new print. Continue re-copying in this
way until you have the quality that
you want.
A second less time-consuming way
to make a line print is to use special
35mm Ortho film Type 3 (about 1.25
ASA) made by Kodak.

MALCOLM SCOULAR

Contact your negative on to a strip
of this film. Process this inter-
positive in an ordinary lith developer.
When dry, contact it on to another
strip and process this negative in
the same way. Any grade of paper can
be used to produce a completely black/
white print from this final negative.
Solarization is another technique
which can produce fascinating results
in the darkroom. The method is
simple; the difficulty lies in its
unpredictability.
One method for black and white prints
is to expose the paper in the normal
way perhaps giving a little less
exposure than the negative requires.
Transfer this print to the developer
and during development switch the
room light on for a second or two.
As the print continues developing,
watch the reshuffling of the picture's
tonal values closely. At precisely

*Apart from the solarized area, bottom,
all effects have been printed by using
various types of screens placed between
the enlarging lens and the paper. Such
screens come with full instructions and
are available from large suppliers, such
as Paterson's who sell world-wide.*

the moment you believe the print to
be right, transfer it quickly to the
stop bath and then the fixer.
After normal fixing, see what
effect the light has made on the
picture. If the print has gone too
far, reduce the time of exposure.
Solarization is a particularly
interesting technique to explore with
nude photography as it will change
the feeling of 'mass' of the shapes in
the picture. If you want to affect only
a small portion of the picture a small
penlight with a narrow beam applied
to the appropriate area will do this.

Framing, Mounting, Cropping

Framing and mounting

A fine photograph does not usually require an elaborate frame, but you can improve an already excellent picture by immaculate presentation. Dry prints can be simply mounted on a stiff cardboard with an adhesive. However, some adhesives contain chemicals which will react with the photograph and damage it. Always avoid using water-soluble adhesives with glaze-finished prints. If you do not require a very permanent mount, use a rubber gum-based adhesive, such as Cow Gum.

Dry mounting

This technique makes use of a shellac-backed piece of tissue which is fixed to the back of a print. This is then placed on the mount and put into a heated press.

It is possible, however, to dry-mount a print without the aid of an expensive press.

Using the tip of an ordinary iron set at medium heat, tack a sheet of mounting tissue to each of the four corners of a piece of thick cardboard. Place the photograph carefully over the tissue and cover with several layers of brown wrapping paper. Increase the heat of the iron slightly and iron over the brown paper covering the print. Work from the centre to each of the four corners. Be sure to cover all areas evenly. Inspect to see that the print is 'taking' evenly to the board. Trim the edges of the cardboard and print flush with the edges of the picture, or leave a border if you prefer.

Difficulties with home dry-mounting are usually caused by uneven heat (causes bubbles), grit between the print and the iron (causes marks), too little heat (the tissue does not not adhere to the mount), too much heat (shellac is scorched and print does not stick to mount), or dampness (the print sticks to the iron).

Dry-mounted prints can be removed from their mounts if it becomes necessary. Consult an expert.

Above and below, the same photograph cropped four different ways for very different effects.

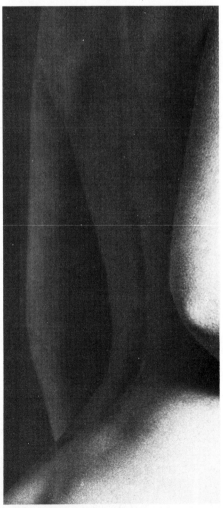

MALCOLM SCOULAR

Pictures That Tell a Story

Photographs which set a scene and communicate something other than pure form, light, or technique are often among those which are the most fun to take.

There is no need to limit photography of the nude to serious figure studies, straight glamour pin-ups, or special-effects pictures. A nude posed in an incongruous setting can sometimes say more than a hundred ordinary poses.

Fantasy is a strong element in pictures of this type. And pictures which interpret a fantasy or attempt to tell a story of some kind are usually very personal. Whatever the idea which inspired the picture, however, the effect will be wasted if the photographer does not ensure that the picture content can be understood by other viewers.

Introducing an element of fantasy into a photograph can mean the difference between an average and an inspiring picture. Fantasy may be found in a carefully constructed artificial scene, as in a studio; or in a completely spontaneous, chance setting, as in the picture at the right.

This photograph was taken as part of a series. It was unplanned and the result which you see here is the outcome of the photographer's quick insight and ability to combine two dissimilar and significant symbols of modern life.

To many people the car is a symbol of power and, in this case, luxury living. The girl appears to have wandered almost accidentally upon the scene and probably serves two functions here. At first she may seem to be the living personification of the car itself, and beyond this, she serves to symbolize the attractions of the car and its implied life-style. Her enigmatic smile is a key to an interpretation of her role. The subdued black and white tones of the photograph add to the feeling that this is an imagined situation.

ROBERT McFARLANE

SPIKE POWELL

A vast number of photographs are
intended for use as illustrations to a
particular story or theme.
The use of props and sets becomes a key
element in such works, but often
those photographs which use only the most
basic props make the most powerful
statements. The two pictures shown here
are meant to convey very different
impressions and both have kept props
to a minimum. Above left, the girl as
a card dealer has a glamorous,
sophisticated look to it and above
right, the girl on the motorcycle depicts
an imaginary association which has
been greatly popularized by the mass
media in films, magazines and posters.

For a successful session such as this striptease sequence, it is helpful for the model to feel relaxed and natural. If she has a sense of humour. the photographer will find it easier to capture a lively, spontaneous atmosphere.

Malcolm Scoular

Photographing a beautiful model doing a strip tease may not be everyone's idea of hard work, although Malcolm Scoular would be the first to disillusion them. He shot the sequence of pictures on these pages — an extraordinarily demanding commission because of the need to make a perfect picture in every frame. Normally, professional photographers have the freedom to bracket exposures and shoot dozens of frames for a single picture, so that if the model moves or the light changes it is not a disaster. The first problem was to find the right model. Scoular says that under ordinary circumstances he would almost certainly have used a professional stripper and shot the assignment with a motorized camera, picking the eventual sequence from hundreds of exposed frames. However, the particular requirements of this job made it essential for the girl to be a professional model: she was going to have to pose convincingly for each separate frame and yet make the sequence hang together. Working to the precise and technical demands of a camera is a good deal different from working for an audience in a strip club.

'Choosing a model for this kind of session is not easy,' said Scoular. 'First of all she has to be someone you can work with, the kind of person who could easily be a friend. It is crucial for there to be a rapport between a photographer and a model. They have to be able to work so closely together that they become almost one person, an indivisible unit.

'Secondly she has to be a girl who is used to modelling in the nude, some-one who is able to use her body in the best possible way and has no inhibitions about doing so. Models who rarely do nude photographs probably wouldn't be able to cope with a session like this — they would freeze and be so tense that it would show through in the pictures. That would be hopeless.'

Having decided on a model, the next step was to write a shooting script which detailed what would be happen-ing in each picture from the first frame to the last. The backdrop chosen for the sequence was a roll of shiny blue PVC which had the gloss of a glamorous setting but did not distract interest from the subject of the pictures.

Scoular, although a freelance, operates out of Vogue Studios and is able to use all their facilities. When such meticulous technical accuracy is required, the processing capability of a big studio is invaluable. It meant he was able to test a complete roll of film and have it processed before shooting any of the final pictures.

For the session, tungsten lighting was used in preference to flash. It had more the feel of club lighting and was more controllable. The latter was important because Scoular intended to introduce a star filter on some of the frames, and he wanted to ensure that the star rays did not cover the model's face. Ektachrome EHB tungsten-balanced colour film was used for both rolls and the camera was a Nikon with a 105mm lens. The exposure had to be changed by a stop at the point where the model was showing more flesh than black dress, otherwise it remained constant throughout. Curiously perhaps, no music was played during the session. Scoular felt that as the strip-tease was to be carried out in agonizingly slow motion and had to be stopped at each frame, it would be better for the model not to be distracted by music. 'It was essential to make the atmosphere as relaxed as possible and the way we did that was through humour. By talking and making jokes all the time, the model can enter into the spirit of the thing and make it fun to do. Obviously you have both got to be professional about it; you must know what you want and the model must know what you want. But if one can surround this with an atmosphere of humour and relaxation, it will create a general feeling of ease. The thing you must avoid is letting the humour take over. You must draw a line before the point at which everyone is having such a nice time that the job becomes less important than the jokes.'

Malcolm Scoular was born in 1947. His original intention on leaving school was to become a painter, but like so many students, art school only managed to convince him that art was not what he wanted to do. 'I became very disillusioned with it all. Fortunately for me I had started to use photographs in my paintings and soon became more interested in making the photographs than the paintings.' He dropped out from art school and joined a big commercial studio as an assistant, where he learned the nuts and bolts of commercial photography. After a year and a half, he decided he knew it all and set up on his own, convinced, as he says, 'that I was going to burst the world with the three decent photographs I had so far achieved.' Much to his surprise, nothing happened. He hawked his three good photographs around to every art director who would see him and got no work at all. With reality rearing its ugly head, he settled down to work at getting together a folio of pictures which would be more likely to convince art directors that he had some talent. When it was finished, he took it to show Vogue magazine and within a few days was invited to join the prestigious Vogue Studios, where he has been ever since.

'Basically I consider myself to be a fashion photographer, although I don't think fashion all the time. I am very interested in taking photographs of women, but my approach is very derivative of my art school training. 'Some of the great painters had a wonderful ability to capture the moment when you get a first glimpse of a woman without her being aware of your presence. It is very immediate and is lost in a few seconds.

'Toulouse Lautrec did it with his bordello paintings. My favourite is of a woman in bed — you just see her head and one arm over the sheets, but to me it is far more erotic than a painting of a completely nude girl. It is as if you have opened a door and seen what is inside as it really is, then quickly shut it again. 'It is this feeling I would like to achieve photographically. But it is very, very hard to do. I think the human body is very difficult to photograph. After all, if you consider it logically, a woman's body is an extremely oddly balanced shape, and it is very hard to get it all 'working'.

Caroline Arber

Caroline Arber climbs mountains for a hobby and takes photographs for a living. She is 30 years old, very pretty, and very concerned about her work. In a tough and competitive profession largely dominated by men, she has carved out a reputation for herself which is growing all the time. 'It's ridiculous,' she says, 'to imagine that only men can photograph girls successfully.' She has proved it. Caroline turned to photography after studying theatre design at art school and working for a year in the theatre. 'I found it very hard getting started in photography because I was a girl.' she said. 'Most photographers want an assistant who can heave heavy equipment about and so they are immediately biased against girls.' Now established in her own right, Caroline finds she is constantly searching for realism in her pictures. For this reason, she always works on location, never in a studio; and finding new and interesting locations is the bane of her life.

The photographs on these pages came about when she heard that a friend of a friend had bought an old gypsy caravan complete with its original interior of mahogany, brass and engraved mirrors. 'It was a perfect place to take nude pictures. I sometimes like to make a story around my photographs and at first thought I would use a girl who looked like a gypsy and shoot a sequence of pictures that would tell a story. But when it came down to planning the session, I realized that there was so much there in the caravan that it would be quite difficult to prevent the environment from taking over. So I decided to use a very young, innocent-looking girl with a slim, pale body, someone who would be in complete contrast to the rich background.

'If possible I like to use girls who have not done nude modelling before. Very often I find that girls who at first do not like the idea of nude modelling will agree to do it for me because I am a girl and they feel less inhibited. From this point of view, it is a positive advantage to be a girl photographing other girls.

'For me, what makes a successful nude picture is for there to be something of the *being* of the girl coming through in the picture and bringing it alive. Some girls are alive in front of a camera and some aren't. Some girls have a natural ability to model which they can improve with experience and feeling for the job. But there has to be some spark there in the beginning. It is very similar to being an actress, in a way.'

One of the difficulties on this session was that the interior of the caravan was so tiny: neither of the two rooms were more than 6 feet square and cupboards around the walls made them even smaller. For some shots, Caroline had to sit on a shelf in order to get far enough away. It meant she had to use a 28mm wide-angle lens most of the time and that some distortion was inevitable. Fortunately, she was able to turn it to her advantage by making the model's legs look longer than they really were. It was very flattering. 'The angles of each part of the body make so much difference to the picture —an awkwardly bent knee or hand can mean the difference between whether the girl looks great or really strange.' All the pictures in this session were

shot with a Nikon camera on High Speed Ektachrome film using available light throughout. With the 28mm lens the exposure was a 60th at f 3.5 and with the normal lens it was a 125th at f 4. High Speed Ektachrome was used because it is rated at 160 ASA and the processing can be controlled. 'You can push this film quite a lot. I tended to underexpose everything and then force it up a bit during the processing. If the transparency is slightly more dense than usual you can overdevelop it by about three minutes to bring up the colours.' Because she always shoots with available light, Caroline normally uses an R10 or an R39 ultra-violet filter to cut out the UV rays from the sun. 'Filters also enable you to play around with different effects without spoiling the actual lens. To get a misty effect, all you have to do is breathe on the filter, then watch through the camera as it clears and shoot at the moment you feel is right. Sometimes, if you are lucky, new pictures present themselves by chance. At one point during the session, the model moved close to the window and I saw what a lovely pattern the engraved glass reflected onto her body' (see the section on Lighting and Moods).

John Kelly

John Kelly says he has had a knack of photographing ladies ever since he took a snap of his gran on the beach and astounded his family not only by getting her all in, but also by getting it so clear. He was eight years old at the time.

Today Kelly is the archetypal successful London photographer with most of the archetypal attributes—a smartly located studio, a flat in town, a Bentley and a cottage in the country. He also has a beautiful wife— none other than Vivien Neves, the best-known nude model in Britain. Viv was the girl who hit the headlines when she appeared in colour but very little else in an advertisement in The Times in 1970. (That particular photograph was not taken by John Kelly, but by another photographer in this group — Michael Boys.) If Kelly fits the image of a fashionable photographer in most respects, there is one area in which he is quite different. He is unhappy when he has to make things happen in front of his camera; his metier is pointing his camera at things that are happening regardless of him.

'What I am trying to achieve,' he said 'is pictures that are good and look as if they are easy to do.'

A very tall, taciturn man, he likes working with girls who are friends, who understand his nature and who don't expect a constant stream of chat and encouragement from behind the camera. Out of his studio, he prefers photographing in the reportage idiom, taking pictures of people involved with what they are doing and unaware of his presence. His favourite picture from an assignment in Jamaica doing a calendar was shot virtually through the loose armhole of a vest being worn by one of the models. She was sitting under a tree on the beach totally involved in something other than being photographed.

'That is the way I really like to work,' he said. 'You see a nice shot and grab it. Sweating in a studio laboriously putting together a picture by telling models to do this is not my idea of photography.'

Kelly's working relationship with Vivien Neves was born out of their mutual independence. 'With Viv you know she has a way of doing the picture that will be right; she is so good at it that you don't have to exercise your tonsils much.

'When I first started getting commissions for pictures of girls, I found it very difficult working with models I didn't know, I just tried to get them to do what they should have been doing anyway and then got on with taking my pictures.

'Some models like to be taken over by the photographer's personality, but that's not my style. Right from the start, I have always waited for my pictures. When I was a student, I used to hang around Liverpool for days with one roll of film, waiting for something to happen.

'Fortunately I soon got to know which girls I could work with. A good model has got to want to do whatever job she is working on and she has got to be able to stick at it. But more than that, there has got to be complete understanding between the photographer and the model and I like that understanding to exist without me having to explain a lot about what I am trying to achieve. I don't think it is important, particularly, whether the girl is a professional model or just a friend. What is important is that you understand each other.

'I was once given two days to shoot eight pages of Viv for a magazine. We did the whole lot in a single afternoon.' We were interested in buying a house out in the country and went up to look at it, taking with us the clothes we needed for the session. We spent the whole morning looking at the house, then when the light had faded a bit we started work.

'I think the picture of her on the bridge is one of the best I have ever taken of her. I like it as a picture, but it has got an added something because I know it was done so quickly and so professionally.'

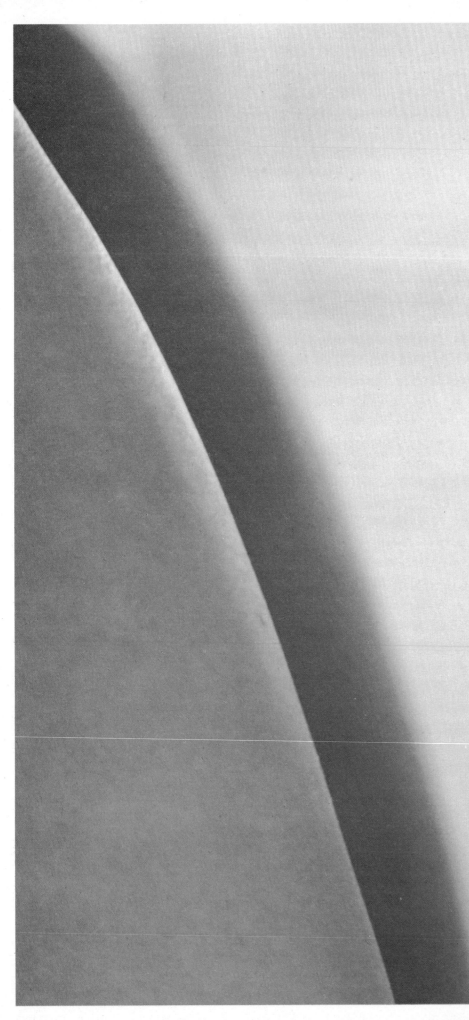

Michael Boys

Michael Boys is one of Britain's
most able photographers. He has
progressed a bit since his early
struggling days; then he felt at somewhat of a loss to convince people
that they should accept his work;
now he finds them clamouring for it.
The success of his very definite
style is often copied. Born in
Burnley, Lancashire in 1930, he was
an academic failure at school but
fortunately was given sufficient
freedom to develop an interest in the
arts, particularly in the theatre and
its technical periphery — sets, lighting
costumes, etc. It was against this
background that an overriding passion
for photography emerged. After
winning a job on a local newspaper, he
learned the finer elements of his craft
from a process engraver, with whom he
shared a darkroom. 'That man taught
me more than any other single person,'
he says. 'Learning how a photograph
is engraved and reproduced is very,
very important.'
Boys is not the kind of man ever to
be satisfied with success. After
working his way through news and
sports pictures to the position of
being a top theatre photographer, he
moved into advertising, specializing
initially in decoration and food
pictures. After publication of his
book, 'English Style', he became one
of the most respected decoration
photographers in the world, and so he
moved on again, this time to photographing girls. Now he estimates that
half his work involves girls and the
other half decoration and advertising.
He has few illusions about his talent.
'I am hired,' he explains, 'for my
ability to capture some feeling of
the transient atmosphere of the
moment. I am not really a graphic
photographer; I am not so excited by
shapes as I am by atmosphere.
'When I am working with nude girls I
am really trying to mix the atmosphere
of sexuality with time and place
and light and the graphics of body

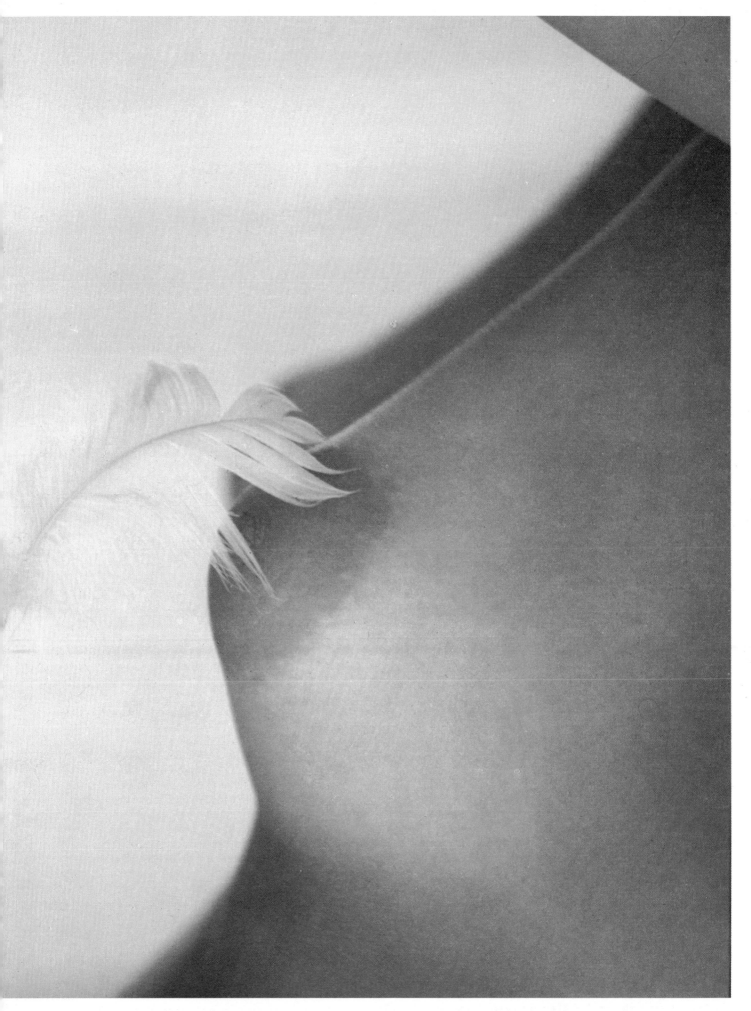

drawing. I am not so much concerned with eroticism. Her nudity, or the perfection of her body, is not significant.

'What is important is that she has got the capacity in her mind to excite, to convey perhaps something of what she is thinking, something of what is happening, or has just happened or is going to happen, something of life as it is at that time. If she can't do that, you might just as well be photographing a string of sausages. The feather picture was one of a series involving feathers and different parts of the body which I shot for a German magazine. The attempt here was to get a feeling of the feather dropping, although in fact we had to stick it in position. Because this picture was shot in my studio I used a filter to counteract the green content of the light coming through the windows. No artificial light was used — all it needed was a white card reflector to fill in. This was shot on Kodachrome II.15th second at 2.8 aperture on a 150mm lens with a 20 magenta filter.

'For the girl in the sand we went to the Sahara. While we were working, miles from anywhere, we heard some noises coming from the other side of

the dune. I went up to the top to find out what it was and ran straight into another British photographer also working with models for another magazine! Apart from trying to find total privacy, the greatest problem with shooting in conditions like these is to keep the sand out of your equipment and to keep the film cool — excessive heat will destroy the quality of the colour. In addition, the exposure meter tends to read the white glare from the sand and consequently gives you a false reading.

'You have to take a reading from the tones you are interested in. The success of a picture like this depends to a great extent on the time of day, choosing the moment when the lines of shadow are right. The effect is also greatly enhanced by turning the camera so that the angle of the dune looks much steeper than it really is. It was shot on Kodachrome II. 500th second at 4.5 aperture on a 300mm lens with a polarizing filter.

'A successful picture such as the girl in the water can only be taken with a girl who has a natural feeling for water. If she loses her confidence in water, it shows. This girl is a Czechoslovakian swimming

champion. Water is her element, she is completely at home and I think you can sense that. To capture the fast movement of the water and the girl I used a motorized camera capable of shooting 36 frames in a few seconds. The filter enhanced the brown tones of the girl's skin and cut out the slightly blue haze from the sun — this was shot in the Alpes Maritime on Kodachrome II. 500th second at 2.8 aperture on a 24mm lens with an 81A filter.

'The final picture (over) is one of my favourites. It has an honesty of mood and an element, of mental depth which I find particularly appealing. You can see there is something going on in that girl's head and it gives you pictures beyond this picture. Part of the relaxed quality is due to the fact that with a film as fast as this (GAF 500), you can work with the camera in the hand and allow the model to move. I used two filters to enhance the colour of the picture heavily towards the girl's red hair. I think this granular sort of film is much more effective if it is not too sharp, so I softened it by spitting on the filter. It was shot at 125th second at 3.5 aperture on a 50mm lens with two filters, a 10 magenta and 85B'.